Christmas Crafts

VIOLAINE LAMÉRAND

TRANSLATED BY:
Jane Brierley

PHOTOGRAPHS:
Bertrand Mussotte

LAYOUT AND DESIGN:
Sarbacane

A word about safety:
Some of the projects in this book require adult assistance. We have marked certain procedures with this symbol. (!)
Make sure to ask an adult for help with these steps.

Scholastic Canada Ltd.

Toronto New York London Auckland Sydney
Mexico City New Delhi Hong Kong Buenos Aires

W9-CTO-256

Table of contents

2

Christmas countdown clock

YOU NEED:
- corrugated cardboard • corrugated paper
- coloured bristol board • scissors
- a craft knife • white glue or a glue stick
- a felt pen • a small plastic container (e.g. for jam)
- clear or masking tape • a needle
- 2 paper fasteners • wire • a pencil
- air-drying modelling clay
- acrylic paints (if necessary)

3 Attach the plastic container behind the window with tape. Pierce the centre with a needle.

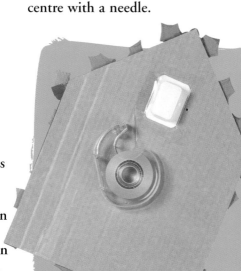

2 With the felt pen, write numbers 1 to 24 on the clock face. First mark 24 on top, 12 at the bottom, 6 on the right and 18 on the left, then fill in the other numbers. Glue coloured paper on the window flap. Write 25 on it.

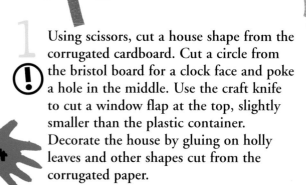

1 Using scissors, cut a house shape from the corrugated cardboard. Cut a circle from the bristol board for a clock face and poke a hole in the middle. Use the craft knife to cut a window flap at the top, slightly smaller than the plastic container. Decorate the house by gluing on holly leaves and other shapes cut from the corrugated paper.

Surprise!
No chance of missing
Christmas with this
calendar clock!

4 Cut a big hour hand from the corrugated paper. Attach it with a paper fastener. Make a spring by winding wire around a pencil. Model Santa's head with the clay, and push the spring into the back. When completely dry, push the other end of the spring through the hole in the plastic container, and secure with tape. For a window lock, cut out a piece of corrugated paper. Attach it with a paper fastener.

Cheery gift wrap

YOU NEED:
- kraft paper • craft foam or flat sponges
- a pencil or pen • white glue
- heavy cardboard • scissors • a glue stick
- a hole punch • crepe paper
- tempera paints • paintbrushes

3 To make a gift bag, cut a rectangle of printed paper. Fold over and crease one long edge to make a finished top opening. Then get a big book and wrap the paper around it, folding up the bottom end, and leaving the finished edge open. Glue the bottom folds and the side seam of the bag.

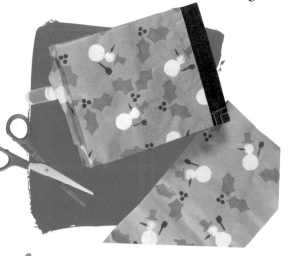

1 Draw designs on the foam and cut them out. Glue them to pieces of cardboard. Now your printing stamps are ready.

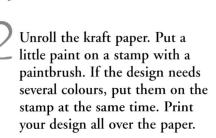

4 Slide the book out. Use the hole punch to make 4 holes (2 on each side of the top). Cut a strip of crepe paper and roll it to make string. Slip the ends through the holes on one side and glue them on the inside. Repeat for the other side.

2 Unroll the kraft paper. Put a little paint on a stamp with a paintbrush. If the design needs several colours, put them on the stamp at the same time. Print your design all over the paper.

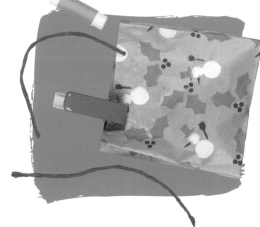

Dream up all kinds of patterns to make your gift wrap unique.

You'll find great ideas for designs in holiday magazines and flyers. Take a look!

Holiday place cards

YOU NEED:
- coloured air-drying modelling clay
- a sculpting tool • black seed beads
- 3 small branches or cinnamon sticks
- white glue • scissors
- a pen • coloured paper

1 Using coloured modelling clay, make the parts for the elf as shown. Press 2 black beads into the head for eyes.

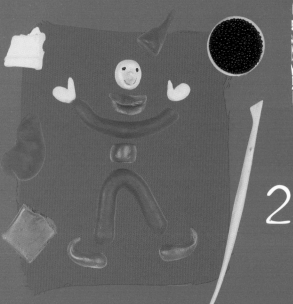

2 Press together 3 small branch segments or cinnamon sticks with a bit of clay. Arrange the elf's legs over the 'logs.' Assemble the rest of the elf, pressing parts firmly together. Let dry well.

3 Make the parts for the snowman as shown. Mould a blanket of snow over the 3 logs to hold them together. Assemble the snowman's other parts, and attach firmly. Let dry well. If the parts come apart after drying, you can stick them together with white glue.

Everyone will find a place at the Christmas table with these cheery helpers!

Dad

Mum

Chris

4 Cut out labels from coloured paper. (Use pinking shears for the elf's "saw.") Add names. Slip labels between the logs and attach them with a drop of glue.

You can also use oven-drying modelling clay such as Fimo. Follow package directions and get an adult's help when you use the oven. ⚠

Jewelled lights

YOU NEED:
- empty glass jars • wire
- cutting pliers
- a tube of gold fabric paint
- flat-backed glass beads
- Plasticine or modelling clay
- transparent glass paint
- a paintbrush

3 Surround the "jewel" with the gold fabric paint. Add other designs, and let dry well. Add other decorations in the same way.

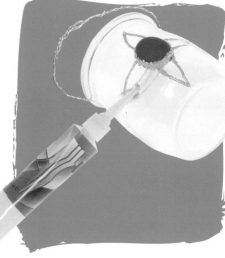

2 Make sure the glass surface is clean and dry. Apply a drop of gold fabric paint to the back of a glass bead and press it on the jar. Let dry well. Keep the jar from rolling with a bit of modelling clay.

1 Cut 2 pieces of wire about 40 cm long. Wind them around opposite sides of the neck of the jar, and where they meet, twist them together to make a handle. Snip off extra wire.

4 Decorate your designs with glass paint. Let dry well.

10

Place these pretty lamps in the window at night to welcome your friends.

Pour a little water in the jar, and float a tea light on it. (!)

Christmas carol wreath

YOU NEED:
- newspaper • masking tape
- green, red, and gold crepe paper
- scissors • cardboard
- white glue • a pencil or felt pen

3 Cut a wide strip of red crepe paper and make a large bow. Attach it to the wreath with another strip. Glue it at the back.

1 Form a wreath with crumpled newspaper. Bind it together with masking tape.

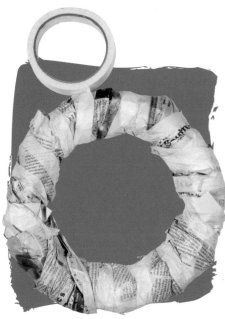

2 Cut one or more wide strips of green crepe paper. Wind the paper around the wreath and glue the ends to the newspaper.

4 Cut narrow strips of gold crepe paper. Twist them to make strings and springs.

Hang this on your door for a musical welcome!

5 Draw musical instruments on cardboard and cut them out. Glue gold crepe paper to one side of the cut-outs, wrapping a bit around the back. Make a treble clef and musical notes with twisted crepe paper. Glue your decorations onto the wreath.

13

Treetop star

YOU NEED:
- newspaper • masking tape • wire
- cutting pliers • wallpaper paste
- tissue paper • scissors • a paintbrush
- white, gold, and coloured acrylic paints
- acrylic varnish (optional)

1 Make a star with crumpled newspaper. Form the points with the masking tape. Cut a piece of wire and make a large spring. Attach one end to the centre of the star.

2 In a bowl, stir 10 mL of wallpaper adhesive into 250 mL of cold water. Let sit for 15 minutes, stirring occasionally. Tear newspaper in strips. Dip your fingers into the paste, then wipe them on a strip. Wrap each point with the wet strips.

3 Twist a strip of tissue paper to make paper string. Dip the string in the wallpaper paste and twine it around the star as shown. Let it dry well.

4 Paint the star with white acrylic paint. Let it dry. Paint again with any colour you like. To highlight the paper string with gold paint, use your finger. When dry, you can varnish the star for a glossy finish.

14

A shining star for your Christmas tree!

Santa's elves

YOU NEED:
- wire • cutting pliers
- styrofoam balls (paint pink if desired) • scissors • glue
- coloured paper • felt pen
- pinking shears (optional)
- polyester or cotton batting

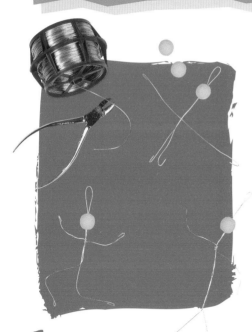

2 Fold a piece of coloured paper in half and cut out 2 layers for the elf's body. Glue them together with the wire between, as shown. Do the same for a collar, cutting a half circle in a contrasting colour. Them cut a single half-circle of paper to make the elf's pointed hat, and glue it on top of the ball.

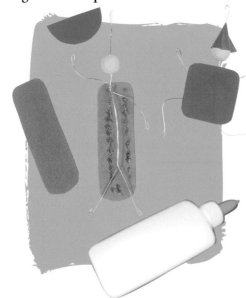

3 Fold another piece of coloured paper in half. Draw elf hands and cut them out. Glue the 2 layers for each hand onto the wire. Do the same for the feet, making boots or pointy-toed shoes. Draw eyes, nose, and mouth on the face, and glue on a cotton-batting beard and hair.

1 Cut a 25 cm piece of wire and fold it in half. Poke the sharp ends through the styrofoam ball, and slide the ball almost to the top, leaving a small loop. Cut a small piece of wire for the arms. Twist it around the wire body. Below, open the wires to form legs. Fold the wires' ends to make hands and feet.

These playful elves can be attached to gifts or hung on your tree.

17

Russian ornaments

YOU NEED:
- corrugated paper in several colours (or white)
- a ruler • a pencil
- scissors • white glue
- tempera paints and a paintbrush (if necessary)

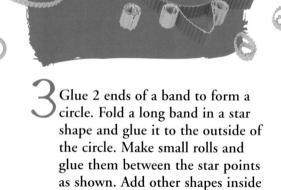

1 If you only have white corrugated paper, paint one side and let it dry, then paint the other side.

2 With the ruler, draw lines on the back of the corrugated paper at right angles to the corrugations. Cut strips of different widths: 2 cm, 2.5 cm, 0.5 cm.

3 Glue 2 ends of a band to form a circle. Fold a long band in a star shape and glue it to the outside of the circle. Make small rolls and glue them between the star points as shown. Add other shapes inside as desired.

4 To make a house, first shape and glue the pointed roof, and glue a large circle inside for support. Inside that, glue other decorative shapes. Beneath, shape and attach another band for the bottom of the house. Glue decorative pieces inside, as shown.

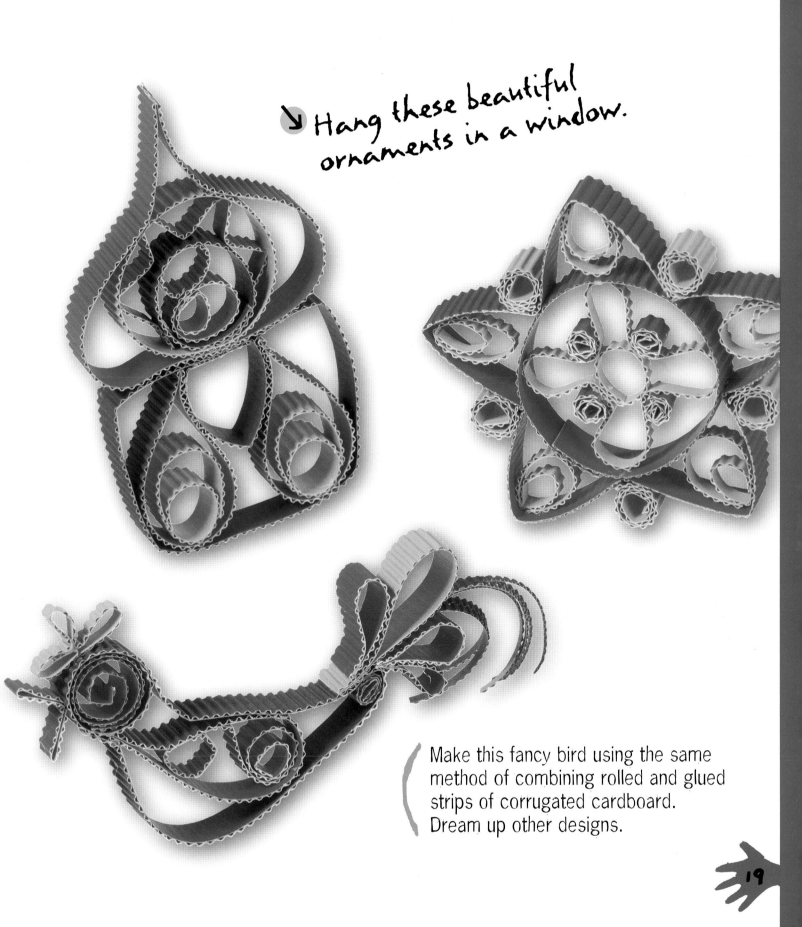

Hang these beautiful ornaments in a window.

Make this fancy bird using the same method of combining rolled and glued strips of corrugated cardboard. Dream up other designs.

Oriental Christmas balls

YOU NEED:
- small round party balloons
- tissue paper
- white glue
- a paintbrush
- gold or silver paper doilies
- scissors
- pinking shears (optional)

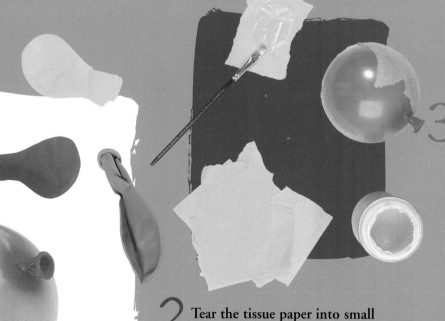

3 Cut strips of tissue paper and twist them to make a string. Vary the thickness by using different widths of tissue paper. Glue strings onto the ball in patterns. Cut shapes out of the doilies and glue them in the open spaces.

2 Tear the tissue paper into small squares and glue them onto the balloon. Make 5 layers in all. Let dry.

1 Blow up a small balloon and knot the end.

4 Hold the balloon knot while pricking the balloon with the scissors to let the air out. Slip the balloon gently out of the ball. Glue a loop of paper string at the opening for hanging.

Blow up the balloons to various sizes for bigger or smaller Christmas balls.

Christmas stockings

YOU NEED:
- 2 pieces of craft foam or heavy paper
- scraps of foam material
- scissors
- a hole punch • a felt pen
- 2 m of narrow ribbon • white glue

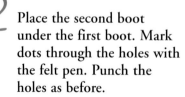

2 Place the second boot under the first boot. Mark dots through the holes with the felt pen. Punch the holes as before.

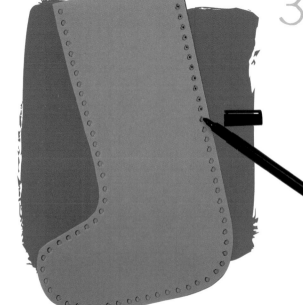

3 Use the ribbon to sew the 2 sides together. Cut out trim for the boot top. Punch 2 holes in the trim and attach it to the boot with the ribbon.

1 Place the 2 sheets of foam or paper together, and cut out a boot shape. Use the felt pen to mark dots 1 cm apart around the edge of one boot shape, except at the top. Punch holes on the marks with the hole punch.

Cut out decorative shapes from foam or paper, and glue them onto the boot. Punch a hole on the back of the boot-top and loop ribbon through it for hanging.

Make a Christmas stocking for everyone in your family — even your pet!

Gleaming Christmas garland

YOU NEED:
- an aluminum pie plate • scissors
- a spoon • a napkin • a blunt pencil
- a pin • narrow ribbon
- transparent glass paint and paintbrush (optional)

1 Cut off the edge of the pie plate and keep the bottom. Flatten the plate with the back of the spoon.

2 Put the napkin under the plate and draw Christmas designs on the plate, pressing firmly with the blunt pencil. Remove the napkin and turn the plate over. Outline your designs lightly with pencil and cut them out with scissors.

3 If you have glass paint, apply colours to your cut-outs and let them dry.

4 Make 2 slits with a pin at the top of your ornaments and slip ribbon through them to make a garland.

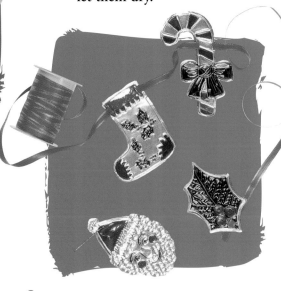

24

Hang this twinkling garland on your Christmas tree or in a window.

You can glue your designs on paper to make pretty greeting cards.

Santa's surprises

YOU NEED:
- a milk or juice carton
- coloured paper • scissors • a glue stick
- a pencil • polyester or cotton batting
- air-drying modelling clay • a table knife
- a toothpick • acrylic paints • a paint brush
- a large needle • strong thread • 12 beads

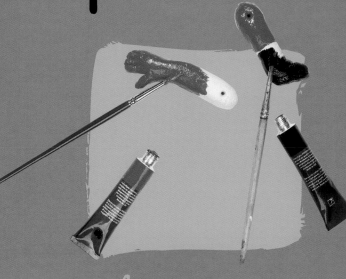

4 Paint the different parts, making sure not to block the holes.

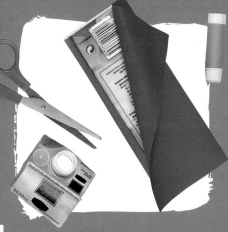

1 Cut the top off the carton. Wrap it with coloured paper, and glue on.

3 With modelling clay, make 2 arms with hands, 2 upper legs, and two lower legs in boots. Make holes as shown with the toothpick. Let dry well.

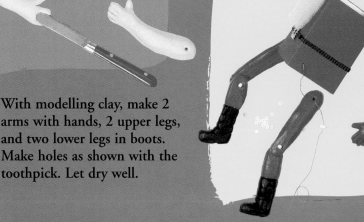

5 Thread the needle, knot the thread, and slide a bead down to the knot. Assemble an upper and lower leg at the knee, knotting a bead on each side. Repeat for the other leg. To attach arms and legs to the carton, use the same method.

2 Draw a head on one side of the carton, and cut around it. Glue on a paper face, and paint Santa's eyes, nose and mouth. Add a fluffy beard, hair and hat trim.

Sit Santa on the edge of a gift or a shelf, and fill his bag with Christmas candy.

Happy holiday scenes

YOU NEED:

- clear plastic blisters (from store packaging)
- bristol board • a green scrubbing sponge
- scissors • white acrylic paint • a paintbrush
- glue • corrugated paper • wire • a pencil
- polyester or cotton batting • bits of wood
- beads, sequins, various small objects for decoration

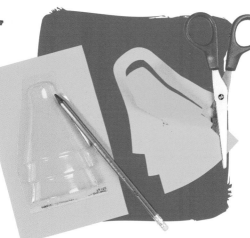

1 Cut bristol board a bit larger than your blister. Cut 2 Christmas trees out of the sponge. Use white paint to add snow to the tops.

2 Make a small cabin with corrugated paper as shown. Make smoke by coiling wire around a pencil. Slide the pencil out, and stick one end of the spring into the cardboard.

3 Glue the cabin and trees onto the brist board. Add bits of wood for a log pile, and fluffy snow. Then place the blister over your scene. Paint snowflakes on t plastic with the white paint. Cut scallo paper strips for a frame, gluing them o the blister.

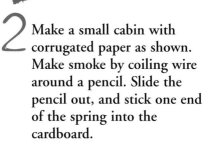

4 If your blister is an unusual shape, place it on paper and draw around the raised part of the blister, pressing hard. Cut out your paper frame, using the pressure marks as a guide. Glue the frame as above.

Give these little scenes as gifts or hang them on your tree.

Tassel Balls

- small round party balloons
- coloured embroidery thread
- wallpaper paste
- gold thread • foil stars
- cardboard • scissors
- a pin

1 Make wallpaper paste by stirring 10 mL of wallpaper adhesive into 250 mL of cold water. Let sit for 15 minutes, stirring occasionally. It should be quite thick. Blow up a balloon and knot the end. Dip fingers in the paste and wipe paste onto the coloured thread. Then wind it around the balloon as shown.

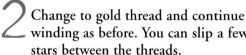

3 When the thread is dry and the ball is hard, hold the balloon by the knot and prick it with a pin. Gently pull it out. Tie a thread to the top.

2 Change to gold thread and continue winding as before. You can slip a few stars between the threads.

4 For a tassel, wind thread around a piece of cardboard 6 cm to 8 cm wide. Carefully remove the cardboard and tie the threads together near one end with another colour thread. Then cut through the threads at the other end as shown, to make a tassel. Slip a thread through the loop, and attach to the bottom of the ball.

30

These Christmas balls are so light that you can make them as big as you please.

Advent tree

YOU NEED:
- corrugated cardboard • scissors
- tempera or acrylic paints
- paintbrushes • white glue
- styrofoam balls (or pom poms)
- 24 wooden clothespins
- gold paper • toothpicks
- a bit of modelling clay

3 Paint the wooden clothespins to create elves as shown, with faces and legs on one side. Number them 1 to 24. If necessary, paint the styrofoam balls, and prop them on toothpicks in clay to dry.

2 Paint the trees with dark paint, then brush on a lighter shade for the branches. When dry, assemble the tree.

1 Cut out 2 same-sized cardboard Christmas trees with scissors. Cut a slit down the centre of each tree as shown: from the bottom halfway up for one; from the top halfway down for the other.

4 Glue the elves on the tree, 3 on each surface. Glue on the styrofoam balls as decorations. Cut out a cardboard star and cover it with gold paper. Use a toothpick to attach it to the top of the tree.

December 25th now seem so far away with a surprise gift every day!

33

Holiday truffles

YOU NEED:
- 200 g white chocolate
- 100 mL 35% cream • 125 g icing sugar
- food colouring • cake and candy decorations
- confectionery cups

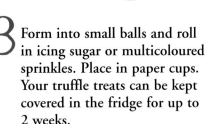

2 Separate the white truffle mix into 4 bowls. Add a few drops of food colouring to 3 bowls and mix well. Cover and chill in the fridge for 1 hour.

3 Form into small balls and roll in icing sugar or multicoloured sprinkles. Place in paper cups. Your truffle treats can be kept covered in the fridge for up to 2 weeks.

1 Heat the cream in the microwave oven at high for 1 minute. Add the chocolate, broken into small pieces, and stir until melted. Gradually add the icing sugar, mixing until well blended.

Leave a few truffles
under the tree
for Santa.
You never know . . .

Yummy yule log

YOU NEED:
- 6 eggs • 300 g sugar • 200 g flour
- 9 mL baking powder • strawberry or raspberry jam
- readymade chocolate frosting • almond paste
  - an electric beater
  - a flat baking pan or cookie sheet
  - a wooden spoon • a clean dishtowel
  - a tablespoon • a table knife • a fork

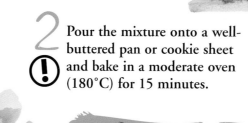

2 (!) Pour the mixture onto a well-buttered pan or cookie sheet and bake in a moderate oven (180°C) for 15 minutes.

3 Turn the cake onto a clean dishtowel. While it is still warm, spread jam on it. Gently roll up the cake. Let it cool, wrapped in the dishtowel to keep its shape.

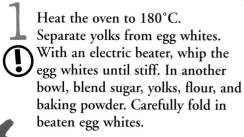

1 (!) Heat the oven to 180°C. Separate yolks from egg whites. With an electric beater, whip the egg whites until stiff. In another bowl, blend sugar, yolks, flour, and baking powder. Carefully fold in beaten egg whites.

A scrumptious cake for Christmas cheer!

4 Cut a slice and place it on top of the cake. Spread cake with ready-made chocolate frosting, except for the cut ends. Draw bark marks along the frosting with a fork. Decorate the cake with almond-paste elves. See p. 8 for elf models.

Santa's workshop

ROOF
8 cm
20 cm

8 cm | 8 cm

SIDE WALL
13 cm
20 cm

END
13 cm
13 cm

Cut paper patterns, using these plans.

YOU NEED:

For workshop
- 3 mL powdered aniseed or ginger
- 3 mL powdered cinnamon
- 175 mL water • 300 g honey • 300 g sugar
- 600 g of flour • 9 mL baking powder

For decorations
- icing sugar • 1 egg white • assorted wafers for roof tiles, shutters, and house posts • candies

2 Roll out the dough and chill it in the fridge. Meanwhile, cut out patterns for roof, ends, and side walls from paper (see plans). Place patterns on the dough and cut out 2 of each.

3 Bake 2 or more pieces at a time in a moderate oven (150°C) for 30 minutes. Cool.

20 cm | 8 cm
13 cm | 13 cm
20 cm | 8 cm

1 Add spices to water and bring to a boil. Add honey and sugar. Stir until sugar is dissolved, and cool for a few minutes. In a bowl, combine flour and baking powder, then gradually add liquid, mixing well to make a dough.

4 Prepare "glue" by mixing egg white and icing sugar in a large bowl. Assemble walls then roof, with this sugar glue. Allow to dry for 2 hours.

38

Cookies and candies make Santa's workshop good enough to eat!

5 Cut ladyfingers in half and glue them on the roof. Add chocolate wafers for house posts. Cut ice cream wafers to make shutters and a door. Glue the candies onto the house. Drip sugar glue on the roof tiles to make icicles.

Thanks to:
papeteries Dalbe and to Rougier & Plé
for their generous help.

First published in French in 2000
under the title "Noël" by Éditions Milan
This edition published in Canada in 2002
by Scholastic Canada Ltd.

National Library of Canada Cataloguing in Publication
Lamérand, Violaine
 Christmas crafts / Violaine Lamérand. --
Canadian ed.
Translation of: Noël.
ISBN 0-439-98982-5
 1. Christmas decorations—Juvenile
literature. 2. Handicraft—Juvenile literature.
I. Title.

TT900.C4L3413 2002   745.594'12
C2002-901143-4

© 2000 Éditions Milan
Photos © Bertrand Mussotte
English text copyright © 2002
by Scholastic Canada Ltd.
All rights reserved.

No part of this publication may be reproduced or
stored in a retrieval system, or transmitted in any
form or by any means, electronic, mechanical,
recording, or otherwise, without written
permission of the publisher, Scholastic Canada Ltd,
175 Hillmount Road, Markham, Ontario L6C 1Z7,
Canada. In the case of photocopying or other
reprographic copying, a licence must be obtained
from CANCOPY (Canadian Copyright Licensing
Agency), 1 Yonge Street, Suite 1900, Toronto,
Ontario M5E 1E5, Canada.

6 5 4 3 2 1   Printed in Canada   02 03 04 05